Canada

Written by

Lionel Bender

Consultant Ann House

Illustrated by

Ann Savage

SILVER BURDETT PRESS
MORRISTOWN, NEW JERSEY

Editor Steve Parker
Editor, U.S. Edition Joanne Fink
Designers Patrick Nugent, Bridget Morley
Photo-researcher Hugh Olliff
Studio services Kenneth Ward

A TEMPLAR BOOK

Devised and produced by Templar Publishing Ltd
107 High Street, Dorking, Surrey, England, RH4 1QA

Adapted and first published in the United States
in 1988 by Silver Burdett Press, Morristown, N.J.

Color separations by Positive Colour Ltd, Maldon, Essex, England
Printed by L.E.G.O., Vicenza, Italy

Library of Congress Cataloging-in-Publication Data

Bender, Lionel.
  Canada / written by Lionel Bender : illustrated by Ann Savage.
    p.   cm. — (People & places)
  "A Templar book" — T.p. verso.
  Includes index.
  Summary: Text and illustrations introduce the geography, history,
people and culture of the second-largest country in the world.
  ISBN 0-382-09508-1
1. Canada—Juvenile literature.   [1. Canada.]   I. Savage, Ann,
ill.   II. Title.   III. Series: People and places (Morristown, N.J.)
F1008.2.B46 1988
971—dc19   87-31163
                                                      CIP
                                                       AC

Contents

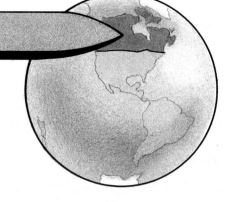

C anada is the second-largest country in the world, after the USSR. It is slightly larger than the United States, its neighbor, 40 times the size of Britain, and more than four times bigger than all 12 Common Market (EEC) countries put together. It stretches nearly a quarter of the way around the globe, over 3,400 miles from west to east, and covers six of the world's 24 time zones.

This huge country contains some of the world's most spectacular and wildest scenery. To the west lie the Rocky Mountains, where Mt. Logan stands 19,850 feet high. To the north is the vast Canadian Shield, a rocky area dotted with thousands of lakes, streams, and swamps. In the far north lie the icy Arctic landscape and the giant frozen islands of the Arctic Ocean. Most Canadians live in the south of the country, because the northern areas are so cold and inhospitable. Many of the main towns and cities are on the fertile lowlands, around the Great Lakes and the St. Lawrence Seaway.

The Western Cordillera
Along the jagged western coastline are rainforests and plateaus. Icefields and glaciers lie in the far northwest. This area borders the state of Alaska.

United States

Yukon

Whitehorse

Symbols of Canada

The red maple leaf is Canada's national symbol and appears on its flag. Before 1965, the

British Red Ensign with the Canadian national shield was flown. The change to the

maple leaf showed that Canadians were increasingly proud of their country.

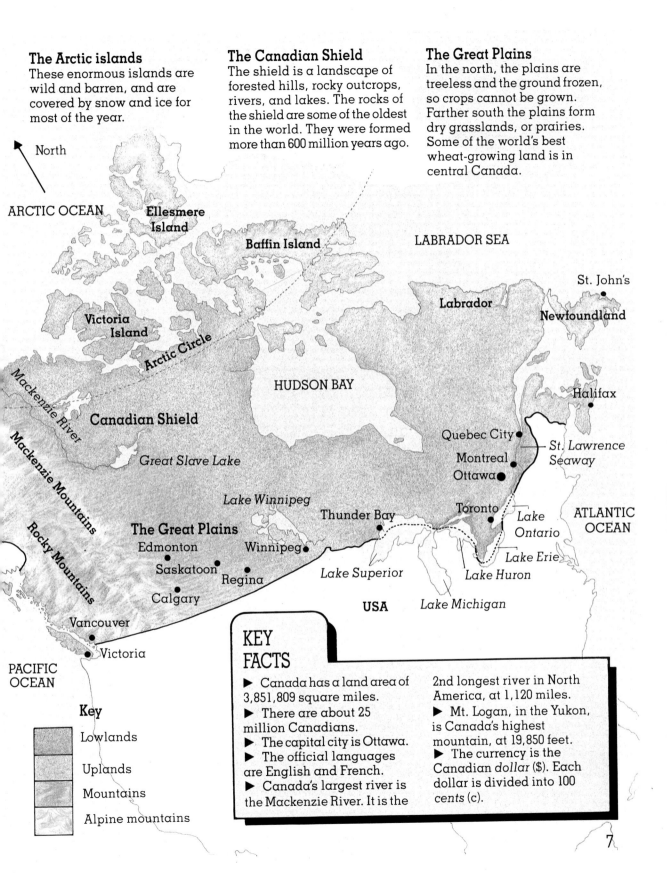

The Arctic islands
These enormous islands are wild and barren, and are covered by snow and ice for most of the year.

The Canadian Shield
The shield is a landscape of forested hills, rocky outcrops, rivers, and lakes. The rocks of the shield are some of the oldest in the world. They were formed more than 600 million years ago.

The Great Plains
In the north, the plains are treeless and the ground frozen, so crops cannot be grown. Farther south the plains form dry grasslands, or prairies. Some of the world's best wheat-growing land is in central Canada.

North

ARCTIC OCEAN

Ellesmere Island

Baffin Island

LABRADOR SEA

St. John's

Labrador

Newfoundland

Victoria Island

Arctic Circle

Mackenzie River

HUDSON BAY

Halifax

Mackenzie Mountains

Canadian Shield

Great Slave Lake

Quebec City

Montreal

Ottawa

St. Lawrence Seaway

Rocky Mountains

Lake Winnipeg

Thunder Bay

Toronto

Lake Ontario

ATLANTIC OCEAN

The Great Plains

Edmonton

Winnipeg

Lake Superior

Lake Erie

Saskatoon

Regina

Lake Huron

Calgary

USA

Lake Michigan

Vancouver

Victoria

PACIFIC OCEAN

Key

Lowlands

Uplands

Mountains

Alpine mountains

KEY FACTS

▶ Canada has a land area of 3,851,809 square miles.
▶ There are about 25 million Canadians.
▶ The capital city is Ottawa.
▶ The official languages are English and French.
▶ Canada's largest river is the Mackenzie River. It is the 2nd longest river in North America, at 1,120 miles.
▶ Mt. Logan, in the Yukon, is Canada's highest mountain, at 19,850 feet.
▶ The currency is the Canadian *dollar* ($). Each dollar is divided into 100 cents (c).

LONG WINTERS, SHORT SUMMERS

L ife in Canada is greatly influenced by the climate. Generally, the spring and autumn are crisp and cool. The summer is short and warm, and at times very hot. The winter is usually long and cold.

In winter, snow may lie on the ground for six months or more. Rivers and lakes are frozen solid. However, homes and buildings are well insulated and heated. Main roads and railway lines are kept open by huge snow-clearing machines.

Spring is the time of the great thaw. Although Canadians manage to continue most of their work through the winter, it is a relief when spring comes and brings the country back to life. Farmers can once again work the land and animals emerge from their winter's sleep.

Summer is the busiest time of year for Canadians. Everyone seems to be out and about. In places, temperatures can soar to 104°F. Many offices, schools and homes are air-conditioned. On the central plains, summer may bring heavy storms and tornadoes that damage buildings and crops.

Autumn is very colorful as the leaves on the trees turn shades of red, gold, yellow, and brown. Often there is a warm spell, or "Indian summer", during autumn. Some people enjoy a late vacation at this time, before the winter sets in.

KEY FACTS

► In Montreal, January temperatures average 23°F. In July the average is 70°F.
► In the far north, winter temperatures can fall to as low as minus 80°F.
► In the summer, temperatures in the south may reach over 100°F.
► In 1987 a tornado struck Edmonton, killing 26 people and injuring 250.
► The chinook is a warm wind that blows eastward from the Rocky Mountains. It can raise lowland temperatures from sub-zero to well above freezing in a few hours. This can cause sudden thaws and massive flooding.

Weather report
In 1980 Canada had a long, hot, dry spell in late summer. The damage caused by forest fires and the loss of crops due to lack of water cost the country more than three billion dollars.

Winter clothing

Before stepping outside into the Canadian winter, it is essential to be dressed properly. People wear warm boots, gloves, a hat with ear flaps, and a thick overcoat or parka. "Parka" is an Inuit (Eskimo) word, used for the caribou-skin winter clothing worn by these northern people. This word is now used for many types of furry-hooded coats, as shown here.

Flowers in winter

The west coast of Canada has the mildest conditions. The average temperature in January is 37°F, and in July it is 64°F. There is also plenty of rain. Plants have been known to flower at Christmas in Vancouver. These winter flowers are in Butchart Gardens, Victoria.

THE TEN PROVINCES

During the 18th and 19th centuries, Canada was a country of scattered and remote settlements. Travel was slow, and often impossible in winter. Then the Canadian Pacific Railway was completed in 1885, running from coast to coast. The settlements were united and people could travel across the nation.

Today, Canada is an independent country. It is part of the British Commonwealth, and the British Queen is Head of State. The Canadian nation is made up of 10 provinces and two territories. Each province has its own provincial government and controls many of its own affairs, such as highways and education. Quebec, Ontario, Nova Scotia, and New Brunswick were the first provinces to join together to form a single Government of Canada, in 1867. Within four years, Manitoba and British Columbia also joined and the new Canada stretched from sea to sea. By 1905, Prince Edward Island, Saskatchewan and Alberta were added. In 1949 the 10th province, Newfoundland, joined.

First and last
Newfoundland became Britain's first colony when the explorer John Cabot landed there in 1497. King Henry VII of England had sent Cabot to discover new lands and find fabulous riches. Cabot (above) thought that he had reached the northeast coast of Asia! The King rewarded Cabot with 10 golden guineas for the "New Found Land". In 1949, Newfoundland became the last province to join the Canadian Confederation.

The Mounties
In the 1870s, settlers started to move overland into western Canada. The government set up the North-West Mounted Police, to bring law and order to these areas. Known as the Mounties, they quickly gained their famous reputation: "The Mounties always get their man!" They are now known as the Royal Canadian Mounted Police, and they are still the only keepers of the law in the Yukon and Northwest Territories.

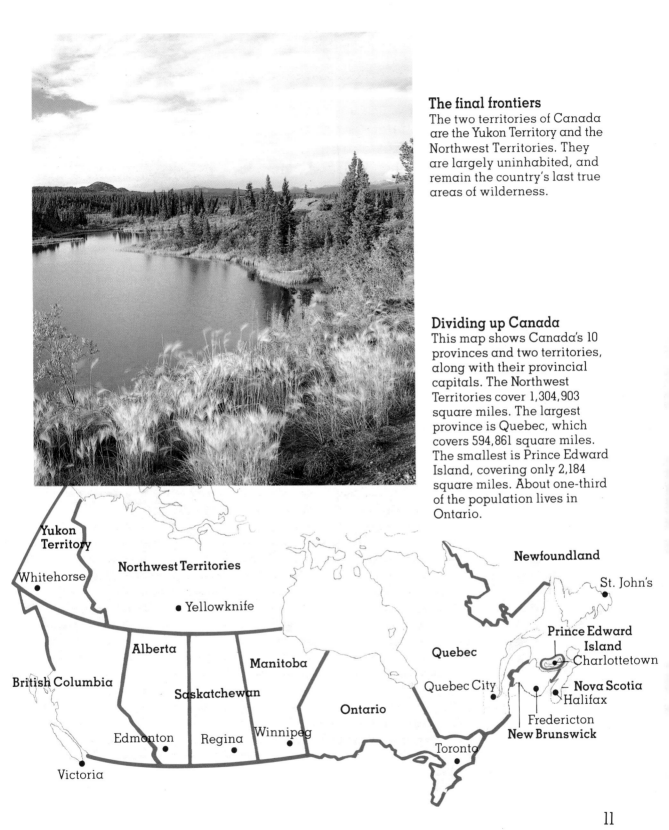

The final frontiers
The two territories of Canada are the Yukon Territory and the Northwest Territories. They are largely uninhabited, and remain the country's last true areas of wilderness.

Dividing up Canada
This map shows Canada's 10 provinces and two territories, along with their provincial capitals. The Northwest Territories cover 1,304,903 square miles. The largest province is Quebec, which covers 594,861 square miles. The smallest is Prince Edward Island, covering only 2,184 square miles. About one-third of the population lives in Ontario.

Yukon Territory

Whitehorse

Northwest Territories

Yellowknife

Newfoundland

St. John's

British Columbia

Alberta

Manitoba

Saskatchewan

Edmonton

Regina

Winnipeg

Victoria

Quebec

Quebec City

Ontario

Toronto

Prince Edward Island

Charlottetown

Nova Scotia

Halifax

Fredericton

New Brunswick

11

FROM PRAIRIES TO ICEFIELDS

There are four main types of wild country in Canada. First is the natural forest zone, which covers almost half the country. Maple and oak trees grow in the east, while coniferous trees such as pines and firs grow in the central region. Moose, deer, bears, beavers, martens, and wolves roam in many of the forests.

Second is the Arctic tundra. Here, it is too cold for trees to grow. The ground is covered by grasses, mosses, and flowers during the brief summer, and by snow and ice for the rest of the year. Caribou are found here in large herds, feeding on the lichens and mosses.

The third type of country is the mountainous areas, with the Rockies in the west and the Appalachians in the east. Mountain animals include bighorn sheep, grizzly bears, and cougars, and birds such as eagles, partridges, and ptarmigans.

Agriculture has largely destroyed the native animals and plants of the fourth zone, the prairies. Foxes, deer, and black bears have learned to live alongside people. However, the endless seas of wild grasses and the great herds of buffalo have long since disappeared.

Hunting as sport

In a huge country like Canada, hunting is possible without wiping out animals completely. However, hunters must obtain a government license and hire guides in many places. The guides make sure that the hunters do not destroy plant life or disturb animals with young. In autumn, many Canadians hunt not only for sport, but also for meat. They obtain venison, rabbit, and moose, to stock the family freezer.

Caribou feeding

Animals of the Arctic

Some of the world's most spectacular animals live on the shores and islands of the Arctic Ocean. Seals, walruses, and polar bears (shown on the right) dive from the ice into the freezing waters. Whales such as the beluga (white whale) still swim here. Sadly, they are much rarer than they were a century ago. There has been very little commercial whaling in Canadian waters since the 1940s.

National parks

The first national park in Canada was created in Banff, in the Rockies. The aim was to preserve and manage the land in its natural state. Now there are 34 such parks. They range in size from the tiny St. Lawrence Islands Park, a group of 18 wooded islands in the St. Lawrence River, to the Wood Buffalo Park on the Alberta-Northwest Territories border. Wood Buffalo has an area of over 27,000 square miles, and is one of the largest nature reserves in the world. It is a safe place for about 8,000 buffalo, as shown here.

13

RICH IN RESOURCES

Canada is rich in natural wealth, from metals, such as uranium, to oil and timber. Some of these natural resources are used by Canadian industry, while huge amounts of minerals and wood are sold abroad. Canada is one of the world's leading producers of nickel, silver, zinc, uranium, and asbestos. Most of these are mined in the Canadian Shield region. Here, too, lie huge reserves of coal, oil, and natural gas.

The country's greatest natural riches include its trees and its water. Forests in the north of Canada provide building timber, plywood and chipboard for use in making furniture, boxes, and roofs.

Canada has one-third of the world's supply of fresh water. The mountain rivers and waterfalls turn turbines to provide enormous quantities of hydroelectric power. Water power is the country's main source of electricity.

Fishing is Canada's oldest industry. For centuries, the Inuit (Eskimos) have caught fish and whales in the Arctic waters. Today, huge fishing fleets sail the coastal waters for salmon, cod, haddock, and herring.

The power of the falls

Niagara Falls, at the northern end of Lake Erie, are on the border between Canada and the United States. Goat Island divides the Horseshoe Falls, on the Canadian side, from the American Falls across the border in the U.S. Both countries have built hydroelectric power stations next to the waterfalls. These turn the energy of rushing water into electricity. The Horseshoe Falls (shown on the right) are 2,600 feet wide and 158 feet high.

Nuclear power

Canada produces all the electricity and other energy it needs. In the 1960s, Canadian scientists developed CANDU nuclear power stations. These run on uranium from Canadian mines. They are among the safest and most successful types of nuclear power station in the world.

The Klondike Gold Rush

In 1896, gold was discovered in the Klondike River area, in the Yukon. More than 100,000 people rushed to the area to seek their fortune. Dawson, in the heart of the goldfields, suddenly changed from an Indian summer fishing camp to a bustling city. By 1910, most of the gold had been found. Here, prospectors wait in line to stake their claims.

Forest of firs

Canada is the world's largest producer of newsprint, the paper used for newspapers and magazines. About half of the newspapers in North America and Europe are printed on Canadian paper. Much of Canada's high-quality timber, used for building and furniture, comes from Douglas fir trees shown here, which can grow to over 190 feet high.

THE FRENCH-CANADIANS

In 1534, French explorer Jacques Cartier sailed up the St. Lawrence River as far as modern Quebec City. He claimed all the surrounding lands for his country, and called them New France. However, British settlers were also arriving. For more than two centuries the British and the French struggled for control of the region. Finally the British won. French settlers were allowed to live in the eastern part of Lower Canada (page 29).

Today, Lower Canada is the province of Quebec. It is still full of French traditions and culture. French is spoken everywhere, written on signs, and broadcast on radio and television. There are French restaurants, stores, and schools. Quebec City, the capital of the province, has the look of an old-world French town. Montreal, the province's biggest city, resembles Paris itself. It is the second-largest French-speaking city in the world.

The Métis

During the 18th century, many of the French fur traders living on the prairies married Indian women. Their descendants were known as the Métis, and they were skilled buffalo hunters. When their way of life was threatened by new settlers, the Métis gathered together and fought back. There were two rebellions, one in 1870 and a second in 1885. In the end, the Métis were defeated by the Canadian authorities. Their leader, Louis Riel (shown above), was hanged in 1885. He is looked upon as a hero by many French-Canadians. Today there are about 100,000 people of Métis descent living in Canada.

Chateau Frontenac

This massive castle-like hotel was built by the Canadian Pacific Railroad and completed in 1892. It dominates Quebec City. It was constructed on the site of the governor's residence. Quebec City is the only walled city in North America.

Montreal

Montreal is Canada's second-largest city, after Toronto. It was founded in 1642, on an island in the St. Lawrence River. It is the center of life in French-speaking Quebec. In 1967, the World's Fair, Expo '67, was held in Montreal. This photograph shows part of "Habitat", a group of 158 unusual houses built for Expo. In 1976, the Olympic Games were also held in Montreal.

Festival of St. Jean Baptiste

St. John the Baptist is the patron saint of Quebec, where most people are Roman Catholics. A festival in his honor is held each year on June 24. It is now more commonly known as *La Fête Nationale*, or National Day. There are bonfire parties and dancing in the streets. Some people even dress up for the occasion as you can see here! In Montreal the celebrations last for seven days.

FACTORIES, FARMS, AND TOURISTS

Canada is a wealthy country and many Canadians have a very high standard of living. This is because Canada has many natural resources. Also, crops grow well, especially on the prairies. Fruit farming is well suited to the climate of southern British Columbia, and the fishing and forestry industries thrive in British Columbia and in the northeastern provinces.

However, in the past 30 years, Canada has also become one of the world's top 10 industrial nations. Processing and manufacturing have become more important than agriculture. One in five Canadians now works in industry – in oil refineries, steelyards and factories, producing machinery, electrical equipment, chemicals, plastics, paper and other wood products, and processed meat and other foods.

One of Canada's biggest growth areas is tourism. Tourists come from all over the world to enjoy the mountain scenery, lakes, and forests. Nature vacations are especially popular. The travel and leisure industry employs more than one million people.

KEY FACTS

▶ Only five percent of Canada is farmed, and only four percent of its people work on farms. Yet more than one-quarter of Canada's economy is based on agriculture.
▶ Three-quarters of Canadian people live in towns and cities. The other quarter live in rural areas.
▶ Canada is one of the world's top producers of cereals.
▶ Two-thirds of the country's factories are in Quebec and Ontario.
▶ One Canadian worker in 10 does not have a job.

The information revolution
Canada is a world leader in electronics, especially in communication by telephones, computers, and satellites. In 1978 the nation introduced Telidon, a nationwide television-and-computer service. In 1981, Telidon was linked to Montreal's daily newspaper, *La Presse*. This created the world's first 24-hour electronic news service in the French language.

The industrial heartland

The industrial heart of Canada is the Great Lakes region. Here there are huge inland ports and manufacturing cities such as Kingston, Toronto, and Hamilton. Giant cargo ships sail across the lakes to the United States. They can also travel via the St. Lawrence Seaway to the Atlantic Ocean, and from there to the rest of the world. Here, grain carriers sit in the frozen water of Lake Ontario.

Wheat to the horizon

The prairie provinces of Manitoba, Saskatchewan, and Alberta contain more than four-fifths of Canada's farmland. Many millions of tons of wheat, barley, oats, soybeans, and sunflower seeds are grown here each year. These grain stores are in Alberta.

WATER, RAIL, AND ROAD

Canada has been able to grow as a nation because it has developed a good transportation system. This has allowed people and goods to move from place to place.

The rivers and lakes were the early transportation routes. The St. Lawrence River made it possible for explorers to travel to the heart of Canada. As early as 1779, canals were built along its banks, so that large ships could reach the Great Lakes.

Montreal, the second-largest inland port in the world, is on this river, halfway between the lakes and the sea. In the north of the country, rivers and lakes are still the main routes for goods in summer, when the water is not frozen.

In 1805, Canada had just 66 miles of railroad tracks. Today, there is a network of more than 60,000 miles. The railways provide quick and efficient transportation for passengers and goods.

Most Canadians travel by road. Almost every family has at least one car. Long-distance bus companies provide the country's most complete network of public transportation. If people are in a hurry, however, they travel by air. Passenger aircraft can fly from Montreal to Vancouver in less than five hours. Small aircraft and helicopters take freight and passengers to remote areas, where there may be no roads or railways.

On the road
The highway system in Canada provides easy access to the more populated areas. The speed limit is 60 miles per hour on main highways and 50 miles per hour on rural main roads. In winter, it is essential to use snow chains on country roads. In the far north snowmobiles must be used instead of cars. Small "skidoos", as shown below, are a common means of personal transportation in many areas.

St. Lawrence Seaway
at Sault Ste. Marie,
Ontario

St. Lawrence Seaway

The St. Lawrence Seaway is a combination of canals, locks and the widened St. Lawrence River. It was completed in 1959 by Canada and the United States. From Thunder Bay, on Lake Superior, to Quebec at the mouth of the seaway, is a distance of almost 2,500 miles. Bulk cargo carriers take wheat and minerals from the lakes to the Atlantic Ocean, and then to countries all over the world.

Four days across Canada

The first east-west railway was completed in 1885. Now it takes four days and nights to travel by rail from Montreal to Vancouver in the west. This train, riding through the Rockies, has an observation car at the rear.

Highway 1

The Trans-Canadian Highway was completed in 1962. It stretches almost 5,000 miles, from St. John's in Newfoundland to Victoria in British Columbia. The highway links Canada's 10 provinces and is the longest national highway in the world.

Highway 1

Banff
Vancouver
Victoria
Winnipeg
Montreal
St. John's

THE PEOPLES OF CANADA

The Canadian population is made up mainly of people of British and French origins. In each of the 10 provinces, except Quebec, English-speaking people are in the majority. French-speaking Canadians, who are known as Francophones, make up about one-quarter of the population.

Canada is quite like the United States. The way of life there is very varied. It has been influenced by many thousands of people from Ireland, Germany, the Ukraine, Italy, the Netherlands, Poland and Scandinavia. Many of these people moved to Canada to find work at the beginning of this century, then settled to raise families. There are also more than 360,000 Native Americans and 25,000 Inuits living there.

Canada has only one-tenth the number of people of the United States, yet these countries are about the same in area. This means that in Canada, on the average, there are only six people to each square mile of land. In the United States there are 64 people per square mile.

The American Indians
These were the first people to settle in Canada, more than 20,000 years ago. The most famous are the Plains Indians, who hunted buffalo. Others were farmers as well as hunters. Nowadays, most of these native Canadians live on reservations, following their traditional ways of life.

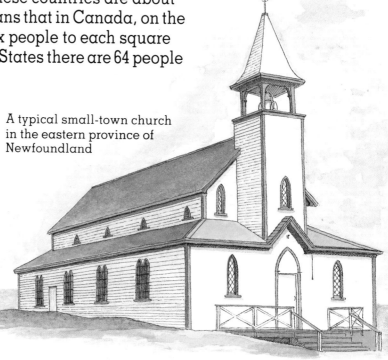

A typical small-town church in the eastern province of Newfoundland

Religion
There is no official religion in Canada. People may follow whatever faith they like. Nearly one-half of the population, including almost all French-Canadians, are Roman Catholic. There are also many Anglican and Protestant churches. Other people follow the Jewish, Greek Orthodox, or Buddhist faiths.

The Inuit

The Inuit (sometimes called "Eskimos") have lived in northern Canada for centuries (see page 26). Recently, their way of life has changed greatly. Today, they often live in houses with central heating and running water. Some still make their living by trapping wild animals and selling their fur or meat, or by working in the small northern towns. These Inuit people from the Northwest Territories are loading their skidoos and sledges for the final hunt of the season, in late May.

THE FIRST CANADIANS

The first people to live in Canada were the American Indians. They came from eastern Asia more than 20,000 years ago. At this time there was dry land between Siberia and Alaska. At first they traveled south along the west coast of North America. Then they spread east and north as the glaciers and ice sheets of the last Ice Age melted away, about 12,000 years ago. Most of these people lived by hunting buffalo, fishing, and gathering wild plants and berries.

The first Europeans set foot in Canada in the 11th century. Viking traders from Iceland and Greenland were followed by explorers and traders from France, Portugal, Spain, and Britain. They were searching for new fishing grounds, new lands to claim for their kings, and a route to the Far East.

Toward the end of the 16th century, the increasing numbers of Europeans brought many changes to the Indian way of life. Many Indians gave up buffalo hunting and began to trap animals for their furs. They traded these furs for horses, cooking pots, guns, and other goods.

Chief Duck of the Blackfoot nation

Gateway to a New World

From about 40,000 to 20,000 years ago, there was a "landbridge" between Siberia and Alaska. It was a wide expanse of tundra landscape, called Beringia. People from Asia settled on Beringia and spread into North America. Gradually the sea covered this land to form what is now the Bering Strait.

The mighty Blackfoot

The Blackfoot people were probably the fiercest of the Plains Indians. They were named "Blackfoot" because their moccasins (shoes) were stained black by the ash from their fires. They were skilled at hunting buffalo, and using spears and bows and arrows. They also made herds of buffalo stampede over cliffs, as a means of killing them for meat, skins, and furs. This hunting was originally done on foot. Horses were not brought to Canada until about 1730.

The Canadian Indians

When white explorers came to Canada, there were many different Indian peoples living there. Historians have identified more than 50 different Indian languages. Here animal skins dry outside a tent-like *teepee*, still home for many Indian families living on the reservations.

Totem poles

For thousands of years, the Indians of the northwest coast have made beautiful carvings, jewelry, and woven fabrics. Many of their patterns have circles, squares, or other geometric shapes. The most famous carvings are the totem poles, which were placed in front of the Indians' homes. The animals in the carvings were of special importance to the ancestors of that family. The word "totem" is from the Indian word for "guardian spirit".

25

THE "REAL PEOPLE"

A bout 4,000 years ago, another group of people arrived in Canada. It is thought that they traveled across the Bering Strait in open boats, and then spread east along the cold northern shores. These people were called "Eskimos" by the Algonquin Indians of east Canada. This means "eaters of raw meat". The people's own name for themselves is "Inuit", which means the "real people".

The Inuit way of life used to be nomadic. This meant they would travel from place to place, fishing and hunting caribou, seals, bears, walruses, and whales. Nowadays, their old way of life has almost disappeared. The Canadian government has bought land from the Inuit to use for mining and oil work. Some of the Inuit have jobs in these industries. However, many of them have no work at all. The Canadian government has recently set up projects to help some Inuit keep alive their traditional customs and lifestyle.

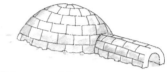

A house of ice
The name "igloo" comes from the Inuit word for "home". It was used for shelter during the long Arctic winter. Igloo camps were built on the thick sea ice of the far north. The hunters kept open holes in the ice, and speared seals as they surfaced for a breath of air. Sealskin was used to make boots. The Inuit made pants from caribou and bearskin and undershirts of fur. Today most Inuit buy their clothes from small stores or trading posts.

Inuit *tupiq* (summer tent)

The summer camp
During the summer months, many Canadian Inuit hunted the migrating herds of caribou. They also used nets to catch salmon and other fish as they swam upstream to breed. Summer dwellings were usually tents of animal skins stretched over a frame of wood or whale bones. Here, the tent and its owner are for the benefit of tourists.

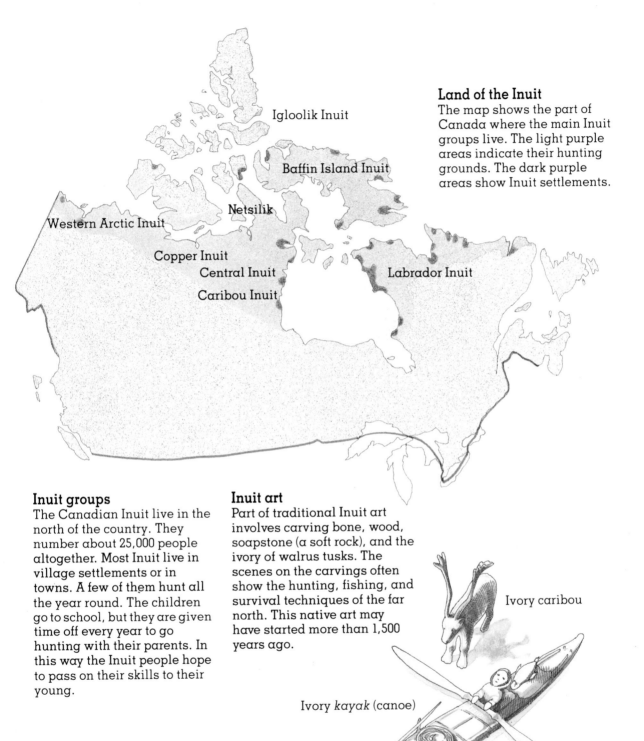

Igloolik Inuit

Baffin Island Inuit

Netsilik

Western Arctic Inuit

Copper Inuit

Central Inuit

Caribou Inuit

Labrador Inuit

Land of the Inuit

The map shows the part of Canada where the main Inuit groups live. The light purple areas indicate their hunting grounds. The dark purple areas show Inuit settlements.

Inuit groups

The Canadian Inuit live in the north of the country. They number about 25,000 people altogether. Most Inuit live in village settlements or in towns. A few of them hunt all the year round. The children go to school, but they are given time off every year to go hunting with their parents. In this way the Inuit people hope to pass on their skills to their young.

Inuit art

Part of traditional Inuit art involves carving bone, wood, soapstone (a soft rock), and the ivory of walrus tusks. The scenes on the carvings often show the hunting, fishing, and survival techniques of the far north. This native art may have started more than 1,500 years ago.

Ivory caribou

Ivory *kayak* (canoe)

CANADA BECOMES A COLONY

By the beginning of the 17th century, Europeans were regular visitors to the east coast of what is now Canada. Their boats fished in the coastal waters and European explorers traded with the Indians for furs.

The French, in particular, were eager to control these rich lands. King Henry IV of France sent adventurers to explore and settle in this country they called "New France". In 1608, the French explorer Samuel de Champlain founded Quebec City. In 1642, the French founded Montreal.

However, British settlers were also arriving in great numbers. In 1670, a group of British merchants set up the Hudson's Bay Company to compete with the French traders. This started a long struggle between France and Britain for control of the region, with its profitable fur trade. In 1759 the British soldiers, led by General Wolfe, captured Quebec City. In 1760 the British took Montreal. In 1763 the two nations signed the Treaty of Paris, which gave Britain control of the North American colonies.

Reaching the Pacific
In 1789 a Scottish trader, Alexander Mackenzie, traveled north along the great river that now bears his name. He hoped to find the Pacific, but his journey ended at the frozen Arctic Ocean. Four years later he followed rivers westward over the Rocky Mountains and reached what is now the town of Bella Coola, British Columbia. He was the first European to reach the Pacific coast of Canada.

Red River Colony
In 1812, a group of pioneers made a long and dangerous trek from Hudson Bay to the present-day Winnipeg area. They traded with Indians on the journey and eventually they came to a place they called Red River. Here they formed a small farming community and set up a trading network. There were battles with the rival North West Company, but the Hudson's Bay settlers did not give up. Red River Colony was one of the first prairie settlements.

Upper Fort Gary, at the Red River settlement, 1870

The Hudson's Bay Company's York Factory (now abandoned), in the southwest of Hudson Bay

The Hudson's Bay Company

This company was set up in 1670 by Prince Rupert, cousin of King Charles II of England. The aim was to trade furs with North American Indians who lived near rivers that flowed into Hudson Bay. Then in 1783 the North West Company was formed by Scottish merchants. The two companies competed against each other. This helped the exploration of western Canada. Today, the Hudson's Bay Company is still Canada's largest fur company. It also trades in gas and oil, and runs many large stores.

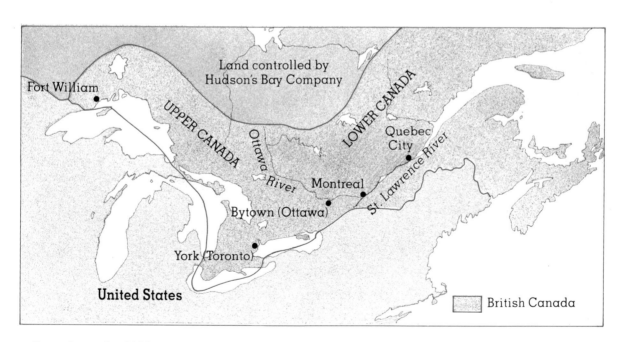

Canada in the 1800s

In 1791, by an Act of the British Parliament, Britain divided its colonial lands into Upper Canada, to the west, and Lower Canada, in the east. The dividing line was the Ottawa River. The French settlers were allowed to live as they wished in Lower Canada, keeping their own language and customs.

THE ROAD TO INDEPENDENCE

During the 1850s, Canadians were becoming louder in their calls for independence. They were still governed by Britain. However, the British believed that giving Canada independence, yet keeping them in the British Empire, would help protect the "British" part of North America from the U.S., to the south. On July 1, 1867 the Dominion of Canada was formed, and Sir John Macdonald became the first Canadian Prime Minister.

The new government welcomed people from all over the world to settle in its vast lands. During the late 19th and early 20th centuries hundreds of thousands of newcomers sailed to Canada, mostly from eastern Europe, to escape the continual wars there. The railroads pushed west and north. New towns sprang up where oil, coal, and minerals were discovered.

Pierre Trudeau, Canadian Prime Minister from 1968 to 1979 and from 1980 to 1984

During the two world wars, from 1914-18 and 1939-45, Canadian factories were busy producing weapons and machinery. This helped Canada's industry and manufacturing to develop. However, by the 1960s, Canadians were worried that they were selling too many raw materials to the United States, and were not keeping enough to develop their own economy. The French-Canadian Prime Minister, Pierre Trudeau, came to power in 1968. His government in particular encouraged Canadians to work for a strong and independent economy, and to be proud of their history and culture.

The New Canada

The Dominion of Canada was established by The British North America Act of 1867. The Canadian government, in Ottawa, was given powers to make its own laws on taxation, trade, national defense, and laws. Each Canadian province had control over its own education, housing, hospitals, and use of natural resources. This system still exists in Canada today.

Sir John Macdonald, first Canadian Prime Minister from 1867 to 1873, and from 1878 to 1891

Political parties

Today, there are three main political parties in Canada. The Liberals and the Progressive Conservatives date from the 19th century, when the Dominion of Canada was formed. The socialist New Democractic Party was formed in the 1930s, following the "dustbowl" crisis of the prairies. This was the time of the North American Great Depression, when millions of people lost their lands and livelihoods.

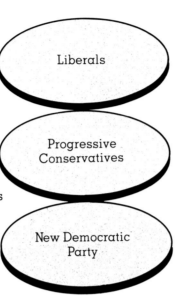

Liberals

Progressive Conservatives

New Democratic Party

The last 120 years

1867 The provinces of Quebec, Ontario, Nova Scotia, and New Brunswick join to form the Dominion of Canada.

1870 Manitoba joins.

1871 British Columbia joins.

1873 Prince Edward Island joins.

1885 Canadian Pacific Railway line from coast to coast completed.

1905 Alberta and Saskatchewan join.

1914-1918 Canada sends troops to Europe to fight in World War I.

1939-1945 Canadian troops fight in World War II.

1949 Newfoundland, the final province, joins the Dominion.

1980 Referendum held in French-speaking Quebec. Should Quebec become independent from the rest of Canada? Most voters said "no".

1982 With the passing of the Constitution Act, Canada is able to change its constitution without involving the British Parliament.

The "dustbowl" crisis

During the 1930s the soil of the prairies turned to dust because of over-farming. Thousands of families like the one above lost their livelihoods during this time.

31

FROM MILL TOWN TO CAPITAL CITY

In 1858, when Canada was still a British colony, Queen Victoria chose Ottawa as the capital. "Ottawa" was the name of a local Indian people, the Odawa, who traded in furs. At that time Ottawa was called Bytown. It was a remote settlement of 7,500 people. But the town stood on the banks of the Ottawa River and at the end of the busy Rideau Ship Canal. This meant it was easy to transport goods to and from the town. Also, it was on the border between the lands of the British-Canadians and the French-Canadians.

Today, Ottawa has a population of more than 800,000 people. It is a beautiful city with many parks, open spaces, and national museums. In the southwest of the city there is an experimental city farm. More than 35 miles of bicycle paths run through the center and out to the suburbs. This makes biking safe, and reduces pollution by cars.

The Rideau Canal is now used for pleasure cruises and water sports. In winter it freezes over and becomes the world's longest man-made skating rink, with more than 5 miles of ice.

Governing Canada

There are two Houses of Parliament in Canada: the House of Commons, and the Senate. The House of Commons is the main governing body. The leader of the political party with the most members in the House of Commons becomes the Prime Minister. The Senate keeps a "check" on the House of Commons. Its members are appointed by the Governor General, usually for their experience in public affairs.

The frozen Rideau Canal

Parliament Hill

The site of the center of government, Parliament Hill, towers high above the Ottawa River. The government buildings were erected here in 1866. Today they are some of Canada's most famous landmarks. At their center is the Peace Tower, which is 312 feet high. An elevator takes visitors to the top, for breathtaking views of the city and surrounding countryside.

Tulip Festival

This is held in Ottawa every May. At this time, the Dutch government sends more than three million tulips to decorate the city. It is to thank Canada for helping Queen Juliana of the Netherlands and her family, when they lived there for a short time during World War II.

ARCHITECTURE AND THE ARTS

Most large Canadian cities are laid out in a grid-like fashion. The streets run parallel to each other and are lined with modern skyscrapers and shopping centers. There are also historic buildings, especially in the smaller towns and villages. These have a traditional feel, with their old-fashioned mansions, railroad stations, town halls, and churches.

Canadians now have more leisure time than ever before. More and more people enjoy seeing films, shows, plays, and concerts, and reading books. In the past, Canada relied on entertainment coming from Europe and the United States. Now many Canadians have themselves become successful in these areas. Each year there are more than 20 major festivals in the country, ranging from children's theaters to wild west shows.

In the 1960s, the government set up The Canada Council. This gives money to people and organizations involved in publishing, music, motion pictures, television, theater, and dance.

Canadian stars
Many of the movie stars, musicians, and other famous people that Europeans think of as "American", are in fact Canadian. They include the actors Donald Sutherland and Michael J. Fox, pianist Oscar Peterson, rock singer Bryan Adams, ballet dancer Lynn Seymour, and TV personality Max Headroom...

A traditional town
Many of the large houses and public buildings in Canadian towns were built in Victorian times, between 1850 and 1900. Some roads resemble an English town, while others look more like a main street anywhere in the United States. The picture above shows the modern towers that dominate the Toronto skyline.

Concert hall

The dome-shaped Roy Thompson Hall is in Toronto. It is a concert hall and theater, and is an example of the modern buildings being constructed in many Canadian cities.

Painting Indians

Paul Kane is one of Canada's most famous painters. He depicted life among the Indians, hunting buffalo and living in tent villages. He painted most of his pictures between 1845 and 1870. This scene shows Indians trapping fish at the Colville Falls on the Columbia River (1847).

CANADA'S CLASSROOMS

In Canada, schooling is free, and everyone from the ages of 6 to 16 must attend. In some provinces, children go to kindergarten from the ages of 4 to 6. Boys and girls go to school together, and have the same lessons.

Each province has its own school system. Some areas have separate schools for Protestant and Catholic children. Except for Quebec, lessons are in English. In Quebec, pupils can choose to be taught in French if they wish. Children taught in English learn French as a second language.

Most young children go to their local school. Older children, and children in rural areas, often have to travel several miles by bus to school. In remote areas, where schools are very far away, children may have to stay at or near the school during the week. They return home on the weekend.

Secondary or high schools may have 2,000 pupils or more. A broad range of arts and science subjects is taught. After high school, students can go to a university at the age of 17 or 18. Or they can go to a vocational school, where they train for a trade or craft.

Education for all
The Canadian government runs special schools for Indian and Inuit children. This helps them to keep their traditional ways of life. In the prairie provinces, more than 20,000 Indian children attend special schools. The schools are usually on the Indian reservations, but they have close links with the surrounding towns. This makes it possible for the children to have a broad education. They learn the same things as other Canadian children, and also about their own history and culture.

Inuit children at their village school

Paying their way

Students at universities and colleges must pay for their education. Some win scholarships that pay for their fees, while others get government loans. Many students are helped by money from their parents. Often, students have to work over vacations and on weekends. They must earn enough to pay their way through college. The picture above shows Queen's University in Kingston, Ontario.

KEY FACTS

▶ There are about five million schoolchildren in Canada.
▶ The country has 272,000 teachers.
▶ The average class size is 17 children.
▶ Young children have the same teacher for all lessons.

▶ When pupils are about 10 or 11 years old, they have a different teacher for each subject.
▶ There are 790,000 students at Canada's universities, colleges, and other places of further education.

FAMILY LIFE AND HOME COOKING

Everyday life in Canada is little different from that in the United States or Western Europe. Canadians are family-loving people. Usually, parents and children have their meals together. Some students live at home and go to the local university. After finishing school young people may live with their parents, until they have been working for a few years or get married.

Men and women are treated equally in employment, and many mothers go to work. In the cities, people live close to the schools, offices, and factories, so they do not have to travel for long periods each day.

Canadians cook well, eat well, and grow foods of the highest quality. A typical meal might be steak, baked potatoes, and salad, washed down with soft drinks or Canadian beer. However, there are many different dishes from across the country. In the west and east, fish and shellfish are popular. In the prairie region, cattle ranchers produce some of the world's finest beef.

Watching and listening

Canadians are keen on radio and television. Almost every home has a radio and a television set. Nearly half of Canadian households have more than one color television! The average Canadian watches 24 hours of television each week and listens to 19 hours of radio.

Eating out

Most Canadians buy fresh foods, not ready-made or processed ones. They also eat out once or twice a week. This is because their country produces such an enormous range of meats, vegetables, fruits, and cereals.

Keeping out the cold

Two-thirds of Canadians live in detached houses and one-third in apartments. Houses have to be built to withstand very cold temperatures. They have central heating, thick roof and wall insulation, and double-glazed windows. Many houses have a basement that can be used as a family room or "den", or as a playroom in the winter. This snow-filled street is in Kingston, Ontario.

Worldwide cooking

Foods from other countries have always been popular in Canada. There are German, Italian, Chinese, and Jewish restaurants and delicatessens in most big cities. Some food markets stock a wide range of Asian, Caribbean, Japanese, and Ukrainian foods. There are also fast-food stores selling pizzas, hot dogs, hamburgers, and fish and chips. These ethnic restaurants are in Montreal.

Regional dishes

British Columbia Crab mousse, lamb with mint sauce, cheddar cheese, cherries, peaches.
The Prairies Chuckwagon stew, buffalo steaks, gamebird pie, Saskatoon pie with cream.
Ontario Lake trout or smelt, turnips and steamed corn with melted butter, apple pie.

Quebec Pea soup flavored with ham hock, *tourtière* (minced pork pie), duck with orange sauce, hotcakes and maple syrup.
East Coast Steamed fiddleheads (ferns) with melted butter, dulse (dried seaweed snack), soused mackerel, blueberry grunt.

A "corn-husking" competition (removing the outer leaves from from corn)

SPORT AND LEISURE

Sports and outdoor activities tend to be divided into summer and winter pursuits. This is because Canada's climate is very different in the summer, compared to the winter.

Football, lacrosse, and baseball are popular with adults and children in the summer. There is great rivalry between teams from the east and the west of the country. In winter, ice hockey and basketball are the main sports. Ice hockey teams play on outdoor ice or in covered arenas. Canadians are among the world's top competitors at ice hockey, skating, and skiing. The nation has produced many world and Olympic champions in these events.

Many Canadians also enjoy tennis and water sports. Nearly everyone lives near a lake, river, or the ocean, or goes there on weekends. Sailing, swimming, and windsurfing are especially popular. Less energetic people play golf, go fishing, or enjoy nature hikes.

The 1988 Winter Olympics
The biggest-ever Winter Olympic Games were held in Calgary, in February 1988. More than 1,500 athletes from 34 countries attended. One and a half million spectators were greeted by the official mascots, the "Welcome Bears" called Hidy and Howdy.

At home on the ice
Ice skating is second nature to many Canadians. Just as European children play soccer and Americans, baseball, on any open spaces, so Canadians practice their ice hockey on the local frozen lake, using boots as goalposts!

The vacation home

Some Canadian families have their own vacation home, often by a lake (as here) or on the coast. Here they spend the hot summer days boating, exploring the countryside, playing sports, and having picnics and barbecues.

Fishing trips

Each Canadian region offers different fish for the angler to catch. The east and west coasts provide excellent sea fishing for giants such as the blue fin tuna (shown here). The rivers of the St. Lawrence area are filled with trout and salmon. Alberta streams teem with pike, perch, and trout.

Blue fin tuna, which can grow to over 13 feet in length.

41

THE CALL OF THE WILD

Canadians enjoy the outdoor life, perhaps because of the peace and natural beauty of the land. On weekends and during vacations, many Canadian people like to escape from the cities and explore and enjoy the countryside. They need a break from the pressures of city living, and from their work in offices or factories.

For many years, places like the Yukon were almost inaccessible and seemed unattractive to city-dwellers. Now, these remote areas are popular with vacationers, tourists, and nature-lovers. Each year, more and more Canadians head north to relive their country's pioneering past.

British Columbia

This western province is famous for its outdoor way of life, both at work and at play. Much of the economy is still based on lumbering, fishing, and farming. The strong and energetic lumberjack is a famous "symbol" of Canada. He can still be seen guiding log rafts down the mighty rivers of British Columbia. The large cities of Victoria and Vancouver are only a short distance from true wilderness. Skiing, boating, hiking, and swimming are more popular here than basketball or baseball.

Skiing – both downhill and cross-country – is a popular sport in British Columbia.

The empty territory

The Northwest Territories are the most sparsely populated areas of Canada. Only 50,000 or so people live in the entire region. About 11,000 of these live in the capital, Yellowknife. More than half the population are Inuit and Indians. These husky dogs and their drivers are taking part in the annual Caribou Festival.

TOMORROW'S CANADA

Modern Canada is a wealthy nation, with one of the most stable governments in the world. Yet the country continues to face problems.

Many foreign companies, especially from the United States, have put money into Canadian industries and businesses. In return, they take some of the profits, and they have a large amount of control over how the businesses are run. Canadians now want more say in the owning and running of their industries. They want their own country to benefit from the profits.

Several issues are still not settled. Some French-Canadians want Ontario to become bilingual (French and English speaking), like Quebec and New Brunswick. Should the Yukon and Northwest Territories be made into provinces? And what about the claims of the Indians and Inuit, who say their lands were stolen and plundered by the Europeans? Their claims are disputed, especially by big businesses, who want to keep the timber and mineral wealth for themselves.

KEY FACTS

▶ The products which Canada sells that bring the most money into the country are motor vehicles and parts, oil, newsprint paper, wood, natural gas, and wheat.

▶ The main imports are motor vehicles and parts, computers, oil, chemicals and precious metals.

▶ Canada sells most of its exports to the United States, followed by Japan, Britain, the USSR, West Germany, and the Netherlands.

▶ Most of the imports are bought from the United States, followed by Japan, Britain, West Germany, South Korea, and France.

Free Quebec!
In recent years, the French-Canadian campaign to make Quebec independent has suffered setbacks. Argument has now shifted to whether Ontario should become a French-speaking as well as an English-speaking province. Here, a dual-language road sign marks entry to Quebec.

Selling to the world

Canada is now trying to trade goods with countries other than the United States. People from Canadian companies are visiting Europe, Japan, the USSR, and South America. They are hoping to persuade businesses in these countries to buy more Canadian goods. Foreign buyers come to exhibitions such as those at the World Trade Center, Vancouver (shown on the right).

A sense of pride

In recent years, the government has offered grants to Canadian companies to build new offices and factories, and to spend more on finding new ways of producing things. Hi-tech areas such as computers and electronics are booming. The aim is to make Canadians proud of their country.

Come to Canada!

Foreign visitors to Canada spend three times as much as they did 10 years ago. Their money is a vital source of income. Canada is now one of the top 10 countries in the world visited by international tourists. They enjoy outdoor sports and some of the world's most spectacular scenery, as shown here.

Index

Acknowledgments

All illustrations by Ann Savage.
Photographic credits (a = above, b = below, m = middle, l = left, r = right):
Cover al Paul Phillips/Zefa, bl Damm/Zefa, ar Hunter/Zefa, br Meyers/Zefa; page 9 a Tourism Canada, b Tourism Canada; page 10 Mary Evans Picture Library; page 11 G Heilmann/Zefa; page 13 a Tourism Canada, b Tourism Canada; page 14 BPCC/Aldus Archive; page 15 a Robert Estall, b K Kummels/Zefa; page 17 a Robert Estall, b Robert Estall; page 21 Tourism Canada; page 23 a Hunter/Zefa, b Sunak/Zefa; page 25 Dr H Gaertner/Zefa; page 26 Tourism, Canada; page 28 a Mary Evans Picture Library, b BPCC/Aldus Archive; page 32 Tourism Canada; page 33 a Robert Estall, b Tourism, Canada; page 34 Danum/Zefa; page 35 a Robert Estall, b BPCC/Aldus Archive; page 37 Robert Estall; page 38 Robert Estall; page 39 Danum/Zefa; page 40 Robert Estall; page 41 Robert Estall; page 43 a Tourism, Canada, b Tourism, Canada; page 44 Robert Estall; page 45 a Tourism, Canada, b Zefa.